PHYSICS

HISTORY OF SCIENCE

PHYSICS

FROM NEWTON TO THE BIG BANG

BY ALBERT AND EVE STWERTKA

A GROLIER COMPANY

FRANKLIN WATTS
NEW YORK • LONDON • TORONTO
SYDNEY • 1986

Diagrams by Vantage Art, Inc.

Photographs courtesy of:
The Bettmann Archive: pp. 11, 20, 23, 24, 64;
The Granger Collection: p. 14;
Richard Cline: p. 26;
The Archives, California Institute
of Technology: p. 48;
Copyright © 1919 by The New York Times
Company, reprinted by permission: p. 55;
Georg Gerster/Photo Researchers: p. 73;
NASA: pp. 76, 77;
AIP/Niels Bohr Library: p. 81

Library of Congress Cataloging
in Publication Data

Stwertka, Albert.
Physics: from Newton to the big bang.

(History of science)
Includes index.
Summary: Surveys the history of discoveries
in physics from the theories of Aristotle
to recent developments, emphasizing the
contributions of Isaac Newton.
1. Physics—Juvenile literature.
2. Cosmology—Juvenile literature.
3. Newton, Isaac, Sir, 1642-1727—
Juvenile literature. [1. Physics—History.
2. Newton, Isaac, Sir, 1642-1727]
I. Stwertka, Eve. II. Title.
III. Series: History of science
(Franklin Watts, Inc.)
QC25.S73 1986   530   86-5669
ISBN 0-531-10224-6

CONTENTS

PHYSICS

CHAPTER

A NEW WORLD OF SCIENCE

In one miraculous year and a half, Isaac Newton made three discoveries that would later shake the world. He was twenty-three at the time and on vacation from Cambridge University, where an outbreak of the plague had forced a temporary closing of the colleges. The year was 1665.

Back home in his native Lincolnshire, Newton was known as a "sober, silent, thinking lad" who liked nothing better than to fasten his attention on problems in "natural philosophy" or science, as we now call it. While he experimented and worked out his ideas, he would often forget to eat and sleep until he had come up with some ingenious solution.

The eighteen months Newton spent in the manor house of his mother's farm at Woolsthorpe yielded a new type of mathematics (later called *calculus*) and a breakthrough in *optics* (the science of light). Most important of all, the experiments of Newton's "miracle year" led to the discovery of *universal gravitation.* Newton's law of gravity, once it had become accepted, remained unchallenged until the early twentieth century. Then Albert Einstein developed his general theory of relativity and thereby laid the foundation for our modern concepts of the universe and its origins.

Newton's life had something of a miraculous quality from the start. He was born in 1642, the year Galileo died, so that it almost seemed as if he came along specifically to continue the great Italian astronomer's work. Newton's father had been dead six months when little Isaac came into the world on Christmas morning. Newton was a premature baby. He is said to have been so tiny that he could have been cradled in a quart pot and so weak that he was not expected to live. A special collar had to be constructed to support his feebly bobbing head. Survive he did, however, to live for many years and to become very famous. He died in 1727 at the age of 84.

While Newton was doing his crucial experiments at Woolsthorpe, the people around him took little interest in his activities, and he was quite satisfied to keep things to himself. In fact, he preferred all his life to work in secrecy and solitude. Nevertheless, after his return to Cambridge University, the brilliance of his ideas so clearly shone through his reserved manner that by the time he was twenty-six he had been made a professor of mathematics.

THE NATURE OF LIGHT

Four years later, the scientific community in London received word that a Cambridge professor named Newton had invented an entirely new kind of reflecting telescope. Eager to examine it, members of the recently formed Royal Society for the Promotion of Natural Knowledge wrote to ask if they could see it. Newton promptly built an improved model and dispatched it to London. This famous telescope became a treasured possession of the Royal Society, where it has remained to this day.

A facsimile of Newton's original
reflective telescope of 1671

Astonished and delighted by the new device, the Academy's members elected Newton a Fellow and asked him to set down an account of his invention in writing. In response, he wrote up some of the optical experiments he had conducted at Woolsthorpe. The account that eventually reached the Royal Society turned out to be far more than a report about a new telescope. It was, in fact, an introductory treatise on optics dealing with the fundamental nature of colors and light.

To begin with, Newton had ground his own lenses. Combining these with prisms and mirrors, he had measured the angles through which sunlight is *refracted* (bent). He had performed hundreds of experiments, taking infinite pains to record his exact observations. His data led him to the conclusion that pure sunlight—white as it may look to the observer—actually contains the entire color range of the rainbow.

This stunning discovery, which went quite against the accepted notions of the time, created a great stir and embroiled Newton in misunderstanding and controversy. Robert Hooke, in particular—a brilliant scientist who was a few years older than Newton—resented the newcomer's idea, in part because it refuted a theory of his own. In his report on Newton's paper, Hooke began by faintly praising it and ended by writing: "But . . . as to his hypothesis of solving the phenomena of color thereby, I confess I cannot see yet any undeniable argument to convince me of the certainty thereof."

Newton so much resented this rebuff by a senior colleague that he waited until Robert Hooke's death some thirty years later to publish his work on optics in definitive form.

PLANETARY ORBITS

A problem that preoccupied many of the Royal Society's members at that time was the great puzzle of planetary motion. Back in 1666 on the farm at Woolsthorpe, Newton, too, had pondered this question. Most of us today are familiar with the story that one summer night the thud of an apple that had fallen from a tree led him to his great insight that the force that pulls an object toward the earth must be the same as that which causes the planets to move. In the same year, without a word to anyone, Newton had even invented a special mathematical system so that he could calculate the paths of the planetary orbits.

Nearly twenty years later, in 1684, the planetary orbits were the subject of a lively debate among several members of the Royal Society. One of them, Edmund Halley, the famous astronomer for whom Halley's comet was later named, took a trip to Cambridge to talk things over with Newton. When Newton mentioned quite casually that he had already calculated the paths of the planets, Halley was astounded. He recognized that he was in the presence of an extraordinary genius, and he persuaded Newton to write out a complete account of his discoveries.

THE *PRINCIPIA*

The prodigious manuscript that eventually reached the Royal Society was entitled *Philosophiae Naturalis Principia Mathematica (The Mathematical Principles of Natural Philosophy)*. Today it is commonly referred to as the *Principia*. Published as a three-part book in 1687, it was written in Latin, like all learned works of the time, and it was illustrated with geometric diagrams. Containing an overflowing wealth of brilliant insights, it was not easy to comprehend. Eventually, the Royal Society published both documents and sent them abroad, as was the custom, to scientists in other parts of Europe. Here again, Newton's discovery caused great excitement, so that he soon found himself bombarded with further questions and objections.

Most of the misunderstandings between Newton and his peers sprang from the novelty of his experimental method. For centuries it had been generally accepted among learned people that nature's laws could best be discovered by thinking deeply about them. An elegant theory had been preferred to an accumu-

PHILOSOPHIÆ
NATURALIS
PRINCIPIA
MATHEMATICA.

Autore *IS. NEWTON,* *Trin. Coll. Cantab. Soc.* Matheseos
Professore *Lucasiano,* & Societatis Regalis Sodali.

IMPRIMATUR·
S. PEPYS, *Reg. Soc.* PRÆSES.
Julii 5. 1686.

LONDINI,
Jussu *Societatis Regiæ* ac Typis *Josephi Streater.* Prostant Vena-
les apud *Sam. Smith* ad insignia Principis *Walliæ* in Cœmiterio
D. *Pauli,* aliosq; nonnullos Bibliopolas. *Anno* MDCLXXXVII.

lation of facts. After all, facts might be accidental and open to change. Newton, on the contrary, had built his case on repeated observation, measurement, and calculation. The doubts expressed by Hooke and others made him angry. After all, his discoveries were the result not of inspiration but of evidence. He thought they needed no further proof.

Even though the letters between Newton and his critics were courteous in tone, he bitterly resented his attackers and begrudged the time he was forced to spend defending himself by correspondence. He wished only to regain his precious obscurity and to work undisturbed. Therefore, a little while later, when the Royal Society again asked him for a paper, he wrote back that he had lost interest in "natural philosophy" and had turned his thoughts to other matters.

The *Principia* was something of a best-seller both at home and on the Continent, which is not to say that all who read it understood it. At least another half-century would have to pass before Newton's concepts were generally accepted and taught.

CALCULUS OR "FLUXIONS"

In 1703, the year Robert Hooke died, Newton at last brought out the full report of his optical discoveries. It was entitled *Opticks, or a Treatise on the Reflections, Refractions, Inflexions and Colours of Light*. In a surprise move, he also included two papers on mathematics in the book. These papers once again demonstrated Newton's genius, but once again they also plunged him into trouble.

It seems that during his famous miracle year, Newton had invented a new mathematical method that he named "fluxions,"

The title page from Newton's Principia, *published in 1687* which was essentially what we now call calculus. For reasons that remain unclear to this day, he had kept the fluxions a secret. His sudden decision to publish them at this late date may have been due to news from abroad. Word had reached him that on the Continent calculus was gaining widespread use and that its invention was being credited to the German mathematician Gottfried Wilhelm Leibniz.

Newton tried, rather clumsily, to show that he had thought of calculus first. Not only that, he later hinted that Leibniz might have derived the idea from him. Although he and Leibniz were acquainted and had always shown the greatest respect for each other's work, they were now drawn into a nasty controversy. Both men had followers, and soon the question of who had discovered calculus became a matter of patriotic pride on each side of the English Channel.

The rather unimportant question as to "who found it first" has never been quite settled. It was clearly an idea whose time had come. In any case, the two great thinkers arrived at it by different approaches. Unfortunately, the quarrel over priority embittered the lives of both men and made the English scientist even more prone to keep his research to himself.

NEWTON'S LATER YEARS

Newton's somewhat crotchety ways and his tendency to be secretive and suspicious may have been aggravated by his total immersion in his work. When he was on the trail of an idea, he cared so little for food and sleep that fatigue sometimes affected his health and spirits. As a young man, he had decided not to marry but instead to devote himself entirely to his studies.

In his middle and later years, Newton read and wrote a great deal about religion and experimented chiefly in alchemy, which was a forerunner of modern chemistry interwoven with mysticism. As we can see from the range and combination of his interests, he may have been searching for a grand unifying principle—some basic set of laws and equations that would reveal the whole mystery of creation.

Even though Newton avoided publicity, all of England venerated him. Among other honors, he was elected a member of Parliament and was made warden of the Mint. In 1705 he was knighted by Queen Anne for his services to science. He served as president of the Royal Society from 1703 until his death in 1727. After his death, another famous Englishman, the poet Alexander Pope, wrote:

Nature and Nature's Laws lay hid in night;
God said, Let Newton be!—And all was light.

CHAPTER

2

ON THE SHOULDERS
OF GIANTS

The story goes that when Newton was in his declining years, a visitor once asked him how he had managed to make so many far-reaching discoveries. The great man replied that if he had been able to see further than others, it was because he had stood on the shoulders of giants.

The giants he spoke of were a few great thinkers who had cropped up here and there throughout Europe in previous centuries and whose ideas glowed like light in the general medieval darkness. Today, when science news travels so fast, it's hard to realize how slowly ideas about the physical universe actually changed in the course of two thousand years of history. In the sixteenth century, though, not long before Newton's birth, Europe seemed to have awakened from a deep sleep and begun to look more closely at the universe and how it functioned. Astronomy, in particular, aroused people's curiosity and imagination. Princes ordered craftsmen to make them intricate models of the earth surrounded by the planets. Societies for the study and advancement of scientific knowledge were founded in Italy, France, and England. Now that we are approaching the year 2000, we can clearly see, as we look back over the last four hundred years or so, that Newton was carried on the crest of a

"On the shoulders of giants"—Aristotle, Nicolaus Copernicus,
Tycho Brahe, Johannes Kepler, Galileo Galilei, Descartes

great new wave of science—a veritable explosion of knowledge that has continued into our own time.

ARISTOTLE'S INFLUENCE

Throughout the Middle Ages and even into Newton's time, the foremost authority on natural science was the Greek philosopher Aristotle. Aristotle's works, originally written in the fourth century B.C., had been rediscovered around the year 1200. His writings on a wide range of subjects were treated as a primary source of information and were consulted almost like an encyclopedia. But although Aristotle was a far-ranging and elegant writer, he had never been a close observer of nature. This had not been considered a fault in his own time, nor in the Christian era, when faith was given far greater importance than investigation. His theories were adopted as truths compatible with the doctrines of Christianity, and the two became so intertwined that eventually to doubt Aristotle's word was to question the teachings of the Church. Therefore, disputations against Aristotle were frowned on in most countries and were sometimes severely punished.

One of the important topics that Aristotle took up in his books was the problem of motion. Why and how did things move? He developed the theory that all objects have their preferred position to which they naturally tend to go. He distinguished between this kind of motion and violent motion, as when objects are displaced by a visible force—for example, when they are pushed or thrown. To explain what keeps an object going after the initial push is over, he supposed it to be driven by the air behind it. As for the movements of the heavenly bodies, he supposed that the sun, the planets, and the stars all moved in perfect circles around the earth. He believed that circular motion came closest to perfection and that the events visible in the night sky were perfect and unchanging forever, quite unlike the constantly changing, imperfect events on earth.

AN EARTH-CENTERED UNIVERSE

After the rediscovery of Aristotle, his followers elaborated a picture of the universe as a system of revolving, transparent crystal spheres surrounding the earth. The stars, gleaming with their own undying fires, were thought to be attached inside those invisible crystal walls. In its symmetry and beauty, this theoretical model had great appeal. But it did not match the actual events to be seen in the night sky. It worked well enough for the stars because they keep a fixed distance from each other and always move in the same constellations. The planets, though, change positions in seemingly inexplicable ways, sometimes even moving backward. The very word *planet* comes from the Greek word for wanderer.

As early as the third century B.C., another Greek philosopher, Aristarchus, had challenged Aristotle's model by suggesting that astronomical events could be better explained by imagining the sun, and not the earth, at the center of the universe. Although this idea cropped up repeatedly throughout the centuries, it was rejected again and again. Common-sense experience seemed to rule that the earth stood still while the sun "traveled" daily from east to west. Besides, the geocentric (earth-centered) universe was the official doctrine of the Church and could not be challenged. The heliocentric (sun-centered) universe was heresy.

COPERNICUS AND THE HELIOCENTRIC UNIVERSE

All the same, nearly two thousand years after Aristotle, a man of great genius, the Polish astronomer Nicolaus Copernicus (1473–1543), had the courage to once again venture a sun-centered model of space. If the beginning of modern science can be assigned a date, it is probably 1543, the year Copernicus's book, *On the Revolutions of the Heavenly Spheres*, was published. This massive volume contended that the earth moves in two different

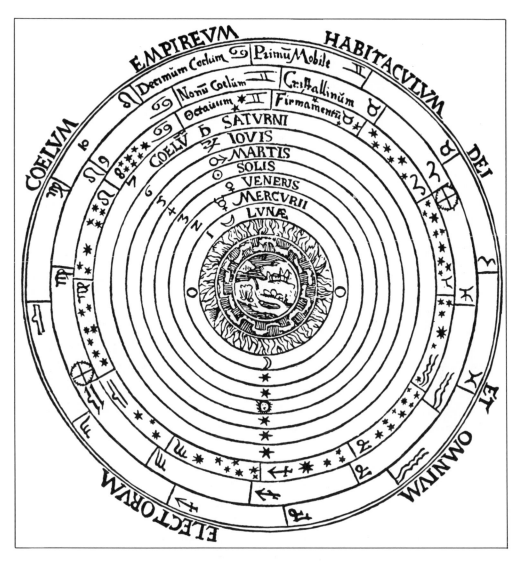

The pre-Copernican universe was geocentric, that is, the earth was believed to be at the center, and the sun, moon, stars, and other planets revolved around it.

The Copernican universe, from an old atlas of astronomy. In this illustration of the helio-centric universe, the sun is at the center, and revolving around it are Mercury, Venus, Earth and its moon, Mars, Jupiter and its four moons, and Saturn. Galileo first discovered the moons of Jupiter, and because they revolved around another planet and not Earth, their existence supported a sun-centered theory of the universe.

ways at once. First of all, it circles around the sun; secondly, it rotates around its own axis. Therefore, he said, many of the changes we observe in the night sky are not real movements but appearances due to the way the earth travels.

Copernicus died the year his book came out, so he escaped persecution. His persuasive reasoning circulated among the learned people of Europe and made its mark. Even though his ideas did not explain everything, they made good sense.

KEPLER'S LAWS

A few years later, the legacy of Copernicus led to another brilliant insight. The atronomer who developed it, Johannes Kepler (1571–1630), combined the Copernican model with calculations carried out by his teacher, Tycho Brahe (1546–1601), one of the last astronomers to make his observations without a telescope. It took Kepler twenty years to analyze his teacher's data. As a result of his interpretations, he proposed that the sun is indeed at the center of planetary motion. But instead of traveling in perfect circles, as had always been assumed, the planets actually move in flattened paths, or ellipses.

This revolutionary discovery, the law of orbits, constitutes the first of Kepler's three laws of planetary motion. The law of orbits further states that the sun is not at the geometric center of the oval-shaped orbit but rather is near one of its ends at a point called the *focus*. The second of these famous laws, the law of areas, states that even though a planet's distance from the sun varies during the course of its elliptical path, an imaginary line joining the planet to the sun sweeps out an area that is always the same in any given time interval. In other words, when the planet is close to the sun, it has to move faster in its orbit than when it is more distant. Kepler's third law, the law of periods, states that the square of the time it takes the planet to orbit the sun is proportional to the cube of the planet's average distance from the

Kepler's Fourth Law:

sun. This is why a distant planet such as Jupiter has a longer year than the earth.

By now, astronomy was becoming a favorite preoccupation among the learned and the great of Europe, and in 1609, Kepler, who lived in Germany, sent some of his work to his Italian colleague Galileo Galilei (1564–1642).

GALILEO'S TELESCOPE

Of all the giants upon whose shoulders Newton would eventually stand, Galileo was the greatest. At the time when Kepler contacted him, in 1597, Galileo was beginning to make a name for himself even outside his own country. But his extraordinary fame was yet to come.

Galileo's ideas on astronomy were consistent with Kepler's. But when Kepler urged him to publicize their revolutionary concepts, Galileo hesitated. He knew how dangerous it was to challenge the teachings of Aristotle, which were held sacred by the Church. Hadn't another rebel and convinced Copernican, Giordano Bruno, recently been burned at the stake for his beliefs? Besides, Galileo was in the habit of working from experimental evidence, and in this case he had too little proof to back up his theory.

In 1609, however, Galileo heard about a handy new device that had been invented in Holland, a spyglass to make distant objects appear close. Spying on the enemy in warfare was the most obvious use for this new technical marvel, which was soon to be named *telescope*, from the Greek words for distant and seeing. But Galileo had a better use for it than that. He constructed an improved model of his own and directed it at the sky.

The things Galileo saw through his first telescope had never been seen by human eyes before. In several different ways, they proved what he and a few others had only been able to surmise. For example, Galileo was able to see the moons of Jupiter, a strange shape around Saturn, and the moonlike waxing and waning of Venus. From watching sunspots change position, he was able to infer that the sun rotates on an axis. Thus, contrary to Aristotle's assertion, he concluded that the heavens are not fixed in rigid perfection, and that even Copernicus had underestimated the complexity of events in space. More was happening out there than just the moon moving around the earth and both of them moving around the sun. Among other things, Galileo could see "four bodies or moons revolving around the planet Jupiter, as the moon does around the earth, while they all, with Jupiter, perform a grand revolution around the sun in a dozen years."

From this moment in history, the notion of an earth-centered universe began to crumble. Although the authorities of the Church prosecuted Galileo for contradicting the official doctrine, many learned contemporaries quietly recognized that he had stated the truth.

THE STUDY OF MOTION

It is often said that whereas Galileo discovered *how* the stars move, Newton discovered *why* they move. To make this discovery, Newton borrowed much from Galileo besides his astronomy, chiefly some famous experiments about the motion of objects that Galileo had performed. It had been Galileo's way not only to speculate about a phenomenon but to set up measurable experimental conditions and to record his observations. The mathematical formulas thus derived from his calculations provided the basis for a new branch of science later to be called *mechanics.*

According to legend, Galileo's interest in motion began when, sitting in church as a youth of seventeen, he used to watch a priest light the candles on a hanging chandelier. When the priest released the fixture, it would swing back and forth. The young man would watch it swing, first quickly in wide arcs, then more slowly in narrower arcs. It seemed to him that even though the width of the swings changed, the time it took for the chandelier to complete each swing always remained the same.

To check out this impression, he timed the swings by his own pulse beats. At home, he tied a weight to a string to construct a pendulum, set it swinging, and timed it again. He found that the time it takes the pendulum to move from side to side does indeed always remain the same. The only way he could change the timing of the swing was to change the length of the string. Eager to earn a little money to support himself in his university studies, he constructed a number of adjustable pendulums and sold them to doctors as devices to measure their patients' pulse rates.

Thus, typically, Galileo's first experiments produced a whole series of important results. Not only had he discovered a basic principle of motion, he had also invented a practical new instrument for measuring time. Most important of all, his method taught his successors how to investigate phenomena scientifically.

Soon afterward, Galileo was intrigued by another idea. Aristotle had asserted that falling objects move faster the heavier they are. This meant that two stones of equal weight tied together would fall twice as fast as a single stone. Others before Galileo had doubted that this was so, but no one had been able to disprove it. Dropping weights from a window was not an adequate test because a free fall is over too fast to be measured precisely.

Instead, Galileo had an inspiration. It occurred to him that he could slow the fall of an object by letting it roll down an inclined plane. By combining downward motion with forward motion, he could observe the objects more easily. He could also separate the two types of motion and analyze them mathematically.

For this purpose, he constructed smoothly polished wooden tracks of various lengths and steepness, as well as smooth balls of various weights. He would release a ball at the top of the track and time it repeatedly along its course.

His calculations proved that Aristotle had been wrong. The

weight of an object makes little difference in its falling speed. Galileo also discovered that all objects speed up as they fall and that the rate at which they speed up is uniform.

MOTION IN SPACE

Galileo never went so far as to relate what he knew about motion on earth to the movements of the heavenly spheres. He still accepted the doctrine that the earth and the skies were subject to entirely different principles. It took Newton, his successor, to perceive the astonishing truth that the laws of physics apply universally, on earth as well as in outer space.

Galileo could hardly have foreseen the far-reaching significance that his discoveries have for us today. One of the ideas that struck him was that if the path of a moving object could be freed of all friction and air resistance, the object would simply continue to move forever. Although the technology to verify his hypothesis was not available in Galileo's time, he was correct. Later, this phenomenon was formulated as the *inertia principle*. Today we make use of the inertia principle when we hurl a satellite into the airless, frictionless environment of space, where its motion will never end.

DESCARTES'S MATHEMATICS

Only one of the giants on whose shoulders Newton lifted himself was still alive when Newton was born. He was the French mathematician René Descartes (1596–1650). It was Descartes's inspired insight that a geometric figure could be expressed in algebraic terms. In other words, one could write an equation for a line with respect to two coordinates, as for example in a graph.

Of course, this opened up a world of new possibilities for translating physics into mathematics. All of today's complex calculations for rocketry and space travel make use of this principle.

Strangely enough, however, when Descartes came to speculate about astronomy, he failed to apply his mathematics to motion in the heavens. Instead, he proposed a theory that some of his contemporaries respected greatly. He imagined that space was completely filled with tiny, invisible particles in constant motion. As they swirled around in great tides and whirlpools, they dragged the heavenly bodies around with them. The most powerful tide flowed around the sun and swept the planets along, while a lesser tide was thought to be dragging the moon around the earth.

In sum, then, this was the state of speculation about motion and space when Newton, as a young student at Cambridge, gained access to his predecessors' work. As yet, no one had put it all together to grasp that physical laws had universal validity, that they could be mathematically formulated, and that humans could use them as powerful tools. It took Newton to formulate this idea.

GRAVITY AND MOTION

Newton's great contribution to the science of mechanics was the discovery that the same laws of nature are valid throughout our solar system. In one grand unifying conception he demonstrated that the force that holds the solar system together and that causes the planets to move around the sun according to Kepler's laws is the same force that produces tides and that causes bodies to fall to the earth. The discovery of the law of gravitation and of the relationship between gravity and acceleration marks the beginning of modern science. There were unfortunately many years between these discoveries and their publication. It has been said that every work of Newton's had two phases: first Newton made the discovery, and then others had to find out that he had done so.

For almost two thousand years, scientists had accepted the laws of motion first stated by Aristotle. These laws seemed self-evident and were backed by his enormous authority. In essence, they stated that it required a force to produce motion. A cart being pulled by a horse, for example, moves because the horse is pulling it. If the horse suddenly stops moving, the cart obviously comes to rest. Why? According to Aristotle, the cart stops because the horse is no longer pulling it, and in one sense, of course, this is certainly true. But Galileo and Newton first realized that the cart stops because something *makes* it stop—namely, friction. This is a very subtle but profound difference in interpreting the same results. It is the force of friction opposing the motion that brings it to rest. Think of the same horse and cart on an icy road. If the horse were to stop, the cart would continue sliding right along.

INERTIA

Before Galileo, most natural philosophers believed that a body was in its natural state when it was at rest. Newton, who carried the ideas of Galileo to fruition, came to realize that motion rather than rest is the natural state of affairs in the universe. An object at rest is simply a very special case of an object moving with zero velocity. What does it take to keep a satellite moving through space? Nothing, just as nothing is required to keep it at rest. This profound insight is called the *law of inertia.* All matter in the universe is inert in the sense that when in motion, it will simply continue moving forever in a straight line with constant speed unless a force acts on it. It takes a force to change the motion of an object.

That it took so long to discover the phenomenon of inertia is probably due to our being accustomed to a world of friction. Slide a book across a table, and it soon comes to rest. It is the frictional interaction between the surface of the book and the table that stops the motion. We have to go a long way from the world of immediate experience, to an atom moving in a gas or a star moving through the vacuum of interstellar space, to observe motion free of friction.

NEWTON'S LAWS OF MOTION

The science of mechanics as we know it today is based on Newton's three laws of motion. These laws were first published in 1687 in Book I of Newton's *Principia.*

The first law of motion defines the concept of inertia. It states that an object will move at constant speed in a straight line forever unless a force acts on it to change the motion. This principle was adopted by Newton from the experimental work of Galileo.

The second law of motion is a more quantitative statement. It states that when a force acts on a body, the force produces a change of momentum. The greater the force, the greater the time rate of change of the momentum.

In everyday usage, to say that an object or process has a great deal of momentum implies that it is difficult to stop. The same is true in *dynamics* (the study of motion and the forces that produce it), except that momentum is defined more precisely as the product of mass and velocity. A change in momentum can be caused by a change in direction as well as by speeding up or slowing down. For example, a car rounding a curve at a constant speed is still undergoing a change of momentum. That a force is required to change this momentum is obvious to anyone who has ever attempted to turn on an icy road. It is the frictional force between the tires and the highway that changes the direction of the car.

What do we mean by the *mass* of an object? Mass is a measure of an object's inertia. The more *inert* (resistant to movement), the greater the mass, and therefore the greater the force needed to change its motion. A bowling ball has more mass than a marble. A bowling ball and a marble dropped from the roof of a building will both have the same velocity when they reach the ground, but the bowling ball will certainly be more difficult—and dangerous—to catch.

The third law of motion states that every action has an equal and opposite reaction. In more modern language, this implies that forces always come in pairs, and that rather than think of some agent exerting a force on an object, it is more nearly correct to think of agent and object "interacting." Whatever the agent does to the object, the object does right back to the agent. There are many familiar examples of the third law. Hit the top of a table with your fist, and the table exerts exactly the same force on your hand. Fire a gun, and there is a recoil.

Newton's laws of motion represent the first great ordering of principles of dynamics in physics. Most of engineering and much of physics today is based on his work.

GRAVITY

Book II of the *Principia*, the least successful part of the work, is devoted to a discussion of various types of fluids and fluid motion. Much of this has since been revised and corrected. It is in Book III that Newton discussed universal gravitation.

Remember the legend concerning the apple that Newton supposedly observed falling from a tree in Woolsthorpe, England, in 1666? According to the well-known French philosopher Voltaire, from whom we have the first account of this apple, "Newton fell into a profound meditation upon the cause which draws all bodies in a line which, if prolonged, would pass very nearly through the center of the earth." What, then, was the cause? Newton's answer to this question was, "Because the earth attracted it." This seems disarmingly simple, but coupled with the insight that the same force might also attract the moon to the earth, it led directly to an understanding of the motion of the moon and the planets.

Scientists before Newton had felt no need to explain the weight of a body or its tendency to fall toward the earth. They were simply properties of all matter. The idea that occurred to Newton and some of his contemporaries, notably Robert Hooke, was that the weight of an object is the result of an attractive force between the earth and the object.

In what is sometimes considered one of the most extraordinary intellectual achievements of all time, Newton saw that a single universal force of gravity could account for the motion of a dropped apple as well as the motion of the planets around the sun and the moon around the earth. The laws of physics were truly universal; the motions of objects on earth and the motion of the stars were subject to similar laws.

UNIVERSAL LAW OF GRAVITY

In the third book of the *Principia*, Newton considered gravitation in very general terms. His reasoning is illustrated by the following example, which he used in order to explain the orbit of the moon. Suppose, he said, we fire a ball horizontally from a cannon on top of a mountain. The ball will be subjected to the pull of the earth, will follow a curved *trajectory* (path), and will hit the earth at some distance from the mountain. If we were now to increase the muzzle *velocity* (speed) of the ball, the ball would travel a greater distance from the mountain before hitting the ground. It is conceivable that we could fire the ball with enough initial velocity so that the ball would never hit the ground but would travel around the earth like a moon. The ball would be a satellite. (See illustration on page 38.)

The next step seemed obvious to Newton. If we can make an artificial satellite in this manner, why not assume that the moon is also constantly falling toward the earth, pulled by the gravitational attraction of the earth? Would this then not also be true for the motion of the planets around the sun? The earth, for example, travels around the sun because it is held in orbit by the sun's gravitational pull. Gravitation, then, is universal.

The gravitational force between two objects gets smaller as the distance between the objects increases. Since both the moon and the apple are accelerated toward the center of the earth by the attractive force of gravity, Newton had a way of finding the strength of the gravitational attraction at the moon. Newton proved that the decrease in attraction is governed by the following *inverse-square law*: the gravitational force varies inversely as the square of the distance between the objects. This means that if the distance between two objects is doubled, the force of gravity falls to one-quarter its former value.

To explain the orbit of the moon, Newton compared
it to the trajectory of a cannonball fired from the top
of a mountain. The ball would be subjected to the pull
of the earth and would follow a curved path. Conceivably,
it could be fired with enough initial speed so that the
ball would circle the earth like a moon.

In his usual fashion, Newton kept the discovery of the inverse-square law, one of the most fundamental laws of the universe, to himself. He did not make it known until the astronomer Edmund Halley visited him in 1684. Both Halley and Robert

Hooke had independently concluded from their own studies that the attractive force holding the planets in their orbits must vary inversely as the square of the distance from the sun, but they couldn't prove it. "What," Halley asked Newton, "would be the curve described by the planets on the supposition that gravity diminished as the square of the distance?" Newton immediately answered, "An ellipse." Halley asked how he had arrived at that. "Why, I have calculated it," replied Newton. When Halley asked him for the calculations, Newton promised to write out all the demonstrations and proofs. Eventually, they became part of the *Principia.*

Why the delay in publishing his results? Although Newton made his calculations in 1666, his results were not published until 1687, when his *Principia* appeared. One of the major problems that faced Newton in demonstrating the inverse-square law was that the earth and the moon are real objects, thousands of miles in diameter, and not mathematical points. What, for example, does the distance between the earth and the moon really mean? Is it to be measured from the surface of the earth, or from the center, or from some other point? Newton made the daring assumption that the earth could be treated for such purposes as if all its mass were concentrated at its center. Without an exact demonstration of this theorem, however, the whole theory of gravitation would rest on intuition rather than on precise calculation. Before he could provide this exact demonstration, Newton had to invent the calculus. Using calculus, Newton divided up the earth into an almost infinite number of small volumes of matter, each attracting the moon according to the inverse-square law, and added them all together to get the total force of attraction. He showed conclusively that his original intuitive assumption, that the earth's gravitational force is the same as if the earth were squeezed into a tiny point at the center, was correct.

Newton finally generalized his views of gravitational attraction into a law of *universal gravitation.* All bodies, no matter where they are located, exert forces of gravitational attraction on each other. The forces are determined by their masses and mutual distances. Triumphantly, he demonstrated that Kepler's laws, the detailed rules governing the motion of the planets that Kepler developed over a lifetime of study, were a necessary consequence of his gravitational inverse-square law force.

Controversy still exists about the extent of the credit that should be given to others for the discovery of the inverse-square law. Robert Hooke actually claimed priority for the discovery of the law of gravitation in a work he published in 1674. The dispute between Newton and Hooke became so bitter that Newton threatened to withhold the publication of the third book of his *Principia.* In a letter to Edmund Halley, who was trying to pacify him, Newton wrote, "The third I now design to suppress. Philosophy is such an impertinently litigious lady that a man had as good be engaged of law-suits as to have do with her." Fortunately, Halley, who generously paid the costs of publication, succeeded in pacifying Newton, and Book III of the great work was sent off to the Royal Society.

TIDES AND PRECESSION

As a further demonstration of the power of this single law of gravitational force, Newton examined various natural phenomena on earth and showed how the gravitational attraction between the moon and the oceans of the earth produces tides. From the observed heights of the tides, he calculated the mass of the moon.

Facing page: *the precession of the equinoxes. It takes about 26,000 years for the earth's axis to circle around once. The two positions shown here are separated by 13,000 years.*

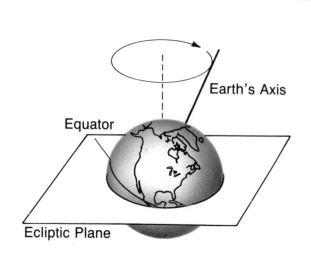

Earth's Axis

Equator

Ecliptic Plane

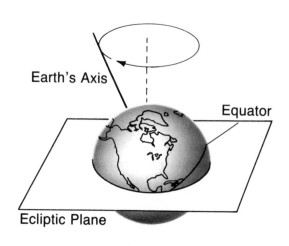

Earth's Axis

Equator

Ecliptic Plane

He also explained how gravitational effects acting on the equatorial bulge of the earth cause the earth to wobble like a top and produce the precession of the equinoxes. We are all familiar with the behavior of a spinning top or gyroscope. Instead of falling on its side under the influence of the earth's gravitational pull, the top slowly rotates around the vertical. The effect is called precession and is predicted by Newton's laws of motion. In a similar fashion, the gravitational pull of the moon and the sun causes the earth to precess around its axis. This phenomenon, the precession of the equinoxes, takes place very slowly since it takes about 26,000 years for the earth's axis to circle around once. It is nevertheless readily observable and causes the celestial poles and equator to slowly alter their positions.

HALLEY'S COMET

Halley's comet is probably the most famous of all comets. Named after Edmund Halley, it is a large comet that can, on some passages by the sun, be seen with the naked eye. Its appearances throughout the centuries, with its glowing tail sometimes stretching a quarter of the way across the night sky, have fascinated and frightened humankind for thousands of years. Because of the comet's appearance in the year 1066, a date known to every English schoolchild as the year of the Norman Conquest, and similar stunning coincidences, there devloped a myth that its recurrence precipitated plagues and other natural catastrophes.

At first, the comet was thought to be a phenomenon associated with the earth's atmosphere. In the sixteenth century, after comets were finally recognized as being of celestial origin, their study was put on a firm scientific basis by the work of Edmund Halley (1656–1742). That the study of comets was close to Halley's heart is evidenced by the dedicatory ode that he wrote to Newton that was included in the *Principia:*

. . . Now we know
The sharply veering ways of comets, once
A source of dread, no longer do we quail
Beneath appearances of bearded stars.

Halley applied Newton's work on gravitation to the comet of 1682. In an "immense labour," he demonstrated that it traveled in an elliptical path similar to the planets'. From what he could learn of the orbits and periods of comets seen in the years 1531, 1607, and 1682, he inferred that they were all the same comet, returning every seventy-six years. "I can, therefore," he wrote, "with confidence predict its return in the year 1758. If the prediction is fulfilled, there is no reason to doubt that other comets will return."

Halley did not live to 1758, but on the night of Christmas 1758, his comet was seen first by an amateur German astronomer, who then alerted other astronomers throughout Europe. Halley had been right, and so had Newton. The appearance of Halley's comet was a dramatic validation of the Newtonian theory of gravity. It ushered in a new age of astronomy and changed people's perception of the space around them forever.

DISCOVERING A NEW PLANET

In the middle of the nineteenth century, astronomers began to notice that the orbit of the planet Uranus was apparently not following the elliptical path predicted by Newtonian physics. Either Newton was wrong or something was disturbing the expected path of the planet. Uranus was then the farthest known planet in the solar system. Making the assumption that a new unseen planet was causing the irregularity, U.-J.-J. Le Verrier in France and J. C. Adams in England were able to calculate the approximate mass of the new planet and where it should be located. Finally, on September 23, 1846, the new planet was observed and was named Neptune. Its discovery was another triumph for Newtonian gravitational mechanics.

ARTIFICIAL SATELLITES

The Space Age began on October 4, 1957, when the Soviet Union launched its first Sputnik into orbit. Within months, American spacecraft were also orbiting the earth. In 1961, President John F. Kennedy announced to the world that it would be a national goal of the United States to put a man on the moon. Under the supervision of the National Aeronautics and Space Administration (NASA), this magnificent goal led to one of the largest coordinated scientific and technological programs the world had ever seen. On July 20, 1969, Apollo II brought humans to the moon for the first time.

There could hardly be more dramatic proof of the accuracy of Newton's theories than present-day space missions. The motion of satellites and spaceships is governed by the same Newtonian laws that govern the planets and the moon. To plan the correct trajectory for Apollo II, the motions and gravitational pulls of the sun, earth, and moon on the spaceship had to be considered. Each moves under the influence of the other. The interactions are so complicated that they would have been all but impossible to calculate without modern-day computers. Behind all this complexity, however, was still the simple and beautiful law of universal gravitation, describing and correctly predicting every aspect of the launch.

BUT WHY DOES IT FALL?

Toward the latter part of his life, Newton suggested various hypotheses about the "cause" of gravity. But the nature of gravitational interaction and its mysterious ability to influence bodies through a vacuum without any contact remained hidden. Ideas concerning gravitation remained essentially Newtonian for the next several centuries. By the twentieth century, a new age of astronomy had dawned, and there was much to explain. Black holes, pulsars, gravity waves, and an expanding universe threatened to topple the supremacy of Newton's ideas.

Other surprises came from the field of particle physics. Recently, for example, a group of scientists suggested the possibility of a new force—a force different from the four known forces thought to govern the behavior of all matter in the universe. This so-called "fifth force" would cause the earth to repel objects within approximately 600 feet (183 m) of the earth's surface and therefore oppose the force of gravity attracting them. The amount of repulsion would depend on the atomic structure of the material. Galileo's famous observation that all freely falling bodies accelerate at the same rate would then no longer be true. Rather, a steel ball would fall to the earth more slowly than a wooden ball because the theory predicts that the "fifth force" would cause the earth to repel iron more than wood. Is this theory valid? Researchers using lasers and delicate magnetic fields are looking for further evidence.

The possible existence of a "fifth force" does not alter Newton's original concept of gravity. It was Albert Einstein, two hundred years after Newton, who took the next step. His general theory of relativity represented a radically new attempt to understand the nature of gravity. We shall consider his ideas in the next chapter.

CHAPTER

4

NEWTON
AND EINSTEIN

The profound admiration that Einstein felt for Newton is best expressed in Einstein's own words: "In one person he combined the experimenter, the theorist, the mechanic, and not least, the artist in exposition. He stands before us strong, certain, and alone: his joy in creation and his minute precision are evident in every word and every figure." He spoke of the wonderful events that the great Newton experienced in his young days and the "deep veneration his achievements deserve."

Reverent as Einstein was, however, there were some differences in how the two men conceived of the scientific method. Newton believed that scientific progress was based on experiments and empirical observations. *Hypotheses non fingo*—I frame no hypotheses—was Newton's famous dictum. One could almost think of this as the keystone of scientific thought throughout the nineteenth century. Experience, and experience only, guided the creation of concepts and ideas.

With Einstein, the grand conception came first, and then—it was to be hoped—came the experimental evidence that would confirm the new idea. The special theory of relativity, for example, is almost entirely based on free invention and Einstein's famous *Gedanken*, or "thought," experiments. Only after its creation was relativity confronted with reality. "Newton, forgive

me," he wrote, "you found the only way which in your age was just about possible for a man with the highest powers of thought and creativity. The concepts which you created are guiding our thinking in physics even today, although we now know that they will have to be replaced by others farther removed from the sphere of immediate experience, if we aim at a profounder understanding of relationships."

CAUSALITY

The ability to predict the outcome of a certain sequence of events is basic to classical reasoning in science. Known as the *principle of causality*, or cause and effect, it seems almost too obvious to bother with. A baseball is hit with a bat, and the ball flies off in a well-defined trajectory. If we know the angle of the ball and its speed after it leaves the bat, we can predict the exact position of the ball at any future time. Our ability to describe the ball's path depends on our having enough information to use Newton's laws of motion. Given the correct data, then, the rest is simply cause and effect.

At the beginning of the twentieth century, however, physicists probing the world of the atom discovered that Newtonian ideas were inadequate to explain what they were observing. It was the quantum theory, one of the most successful of moden scientific ideas, that became the interpreter of atomic and particle physics. Developed during the 1920s by the celebrated scientists Werner Heisenberg and Niels Bohr, the quantum theory proclaimed the death of causality. It was no longer possible simultaneously to predict the position and velocity of an atom with unlimited precision. Even more startling, perhaps, was the idea that the very outcome of some experiments was uncertain and not entirely

Albert Einstein

predictable. The path of a moving electron reflected off a metal surface was, for example, incapable of being precisely known. It might bounce into a detector at an angle of 30 degrees, but it might also bounce at an angle of 45 degrees. Quantum theory tells us only the probability of each of these events occurring. It is the experiment itself that tells us which one of the many alternatives actually occurred. Chance rather than certainty rules the world of physics. A radioactive atom might blow up now, but there is also a good chance that it might blow up next month. One can never be absolutely certain.

Einstein was unhappy with quantum theory and never challenged the authority of Newton in the matter of causality. He was fond of saying, "God does not play dice with the universe." In this, he went against the beliefs of almost every modern physicist. "The last word has not been said," Einstein wrote. "May the spirit of Newton's method give us the power to restore unison between physical reality and the profoundest characteristic of Newton's teaching—strict causality."

CONTRADICTIONS IN NEWTONIAN MECHANICS

Einstein's name is, in most of our minds, linked to the concept of relativity. Yet the basic concept of relativity is as old as the mechanics of Newton. Newton's mechanics concerns itself with the motions of particles under the action of forces. Although Newton believed in an absolute space, he also recognized that one cannot describe the motion of a body through this absolute space. Instead, we describe the location of one object with respect to another, usually called a *frame of reference.*

Measurements of the speed of light at the end of the last century produced some troubling and contradictory results. Scientists observed that the velocity of light seems to have a special role in nature. We all know that the speed of a wave with respect to us depends on our own motion. The mathematical statement of this *principle of relative velocities* follows from Newtonian mechanics and is known as *Galileian relativity.* If we are moving in the same direction as a wave, for example, it appears to move more slowly, and if we are moving in the opposite direction, the wave speed relative to ours is greater than when we are at rest. With light, however, this is not true. Remarkably, every observer measures the same value for the speed of light, no matter what their state of motion. Why is this absolute, when all other motion is relative?

Then there was the question of what is transmitting the light. When we speak of the velocity of sound, for example, it is always assumed that the speed of the sound wave is measured with respect to a given medium, such as air. But what is the medium when we speak of the speed of light? Light, after all, can travel through a vacuum.

Even more recently, the development of large particle accelerators raised other questions. According to Newton's laws, there is theoretically no limit to how fast an object can move. As long as there is a force acting on it, the object should accelerate indefinitely, moving faster and faster. Experiments demonstrate, however, that when an attempt is made to accelerate particles to speeds approaching the speed of light, drastic departures from Newtonian mechanics occur. The results are always the same— there is an upper limit to the velocity that may be given to a particle, and this limit is the speed of light.

THE SPECIAL THEORY
OF RELATIVITY

Einstein's celebrated *special theory of relativity*, first published in 1905, marked a complete break with Newtonian ideas of space and time. For Einstein, classical mechanics gave wrong answers because it was based on the untenable assumption of the existence of a universal, absolute time. The profound idea that Einstein brought into physics was that time is no longer to be thought of as the same for all observers. There are as many times as there are frames of reference moving with different velocities. No longer is there to be the concept of absolute simultaneity. Two events that occur at the same time for one observer need not be simultaneous for another observer in a differently moving reference frame.

The theory is based on the now-famous hypothesis that the laws of physics are the same in all nonaccelerated frames of reference, and therefore absolute uniform motion cannot be detected. Although reminiscent of Galileian relativity, it differs markedly in that it also includes the measurement of light. It is remarkable that a revolutionary new theory of dynamics can be based on such a seemingly reasonable and simple-sounding idea. Strictly applied, however, it leads to extraordinary conclusions that oppose our intuitive feelings about some of the most basic properties of nature and that often contradict common sense.

In the Newtonian world, we are accustomed to thinking of space as being measurable without reference to time. Each is independent of the other and simply exists in an unalterable universe. In a similar fashion, we are accustomed to thinking of mass and energy as expressing inherently different properties of a body. The mass of a body was always thought of as being constant and unchangeable. In Einstein's physics of special relativity, however, space, time, and mass are all related and depend upon the motion of an observer.

The first direct confirmation of special relativity was the verification of the increase in mass with velocity that was predicted by Einstein's equations. As predicted, a fast-moving electron in the linear accelerator at Stanford University, for example, has a greater mass than when at rest in the laboratory. Einstein was also able to demonstrate that energy itself has inertia and that mass and energy are interchangeable. The equivalence of mass and energy has become a commonplace idea, and nuclear power plants throughout the world make use of it. The equation $E =$

mc^2, which expresses the amount of energy, E, equivalent to a mass, m, where c is the speed of light, has become one of the most famous equations of the twentieth century—a symbol of relativity and Einstein.

Einstein recognized that his hypothesis had important consequences for measuring time intervals and space intervals as well as mass. His relativity theory makes the astonishing prediction that "a moving clock runs slow." A fast-moving subatomic particle like a "meson," for example, has a different "internal clock" when it is traveling almost at the speed of light than it does when it is at rest in the laboratory. Expressed differently, its *half-life* is longer when it is moving with respect to us than when at rest.

A ten-minute interval for one observer might be only five minutes for another observer in a different frame of reference. A meter stick in one frame might be only half a meter when measured in another reference frame. The changes in such measurements from one reference frame to another are called *time dilation* and *length contraction.* These bizarre results have been verified countless times in laboratories throughout the world. Like it or not, we have to change our ideas about time and space.

THE GENERAL THEORY OF RELATIVITY

The special theory deals only with reference frames moving with constant velocity. How was one to treat accelerated systems, and how, Einstein asked, "was the Newtonian theory of gravitation to be modified so that its laws would fit in the special relativity theory?

"I was sitting in a chair in the patent office at Bern when all of a sudden a thought occurred to me: If a person falls freely he will not feel his own weight. I was startled. This simple thought made a deep impression on me. It impelled me toward a theory of gravitation."

Consider a person standing in Einstein's free-falling elevator.

He would sense no gravitational field, much like the astronauts we have often seen frolicking in their free-falling spaceships. Since all objects in one region of space fall with the same gravitational acceleration, an object dropped in the elevator would appear to remain stationary—there would appear to be no gravitational force at work.

Einstein developed this idea that he called the "equivalence principle" into the *general theory of relativity,* first published in 1915. He soon realized that one of its most important consequences and predictions was the bending of light in a gravitational field. Imagine a beam of light passing from one side of a freely falling elevator to the other. To the observer inside, it would appear to travel in a straight line, but to an observer outside, it would appear to be falling or traveling in a curved path. By the equivalence theory, then, light should also appear to bend in a gravitational field.

Interestingly enough, Newton had already asked the same question in his book on optics: "Do not Bodies act upon Light at a distance, and by their action bend its Rays; and is not this action strongest at the least distance?"

At first, Einstein believed that the bending of light was too small to ever be observed. He then realized that the effect could be detected for starlight grazing the sun during a total eclipse. Using his general theory of relativity, he predicted that the sun would bend the light through an angle of 1.74 seconds of arc (1 second of arc is defined as 1/3600 of 1 degree).

In one of the historic moments in physics, Sir Arthur Eddington, who had led an expedition to Principe Island off the coast of Spanish Guinea in 1919 to observe an eclipse of the sun, announced at a joint meeting of the Royal Society and the Royal Astronomical Society that "a very definite result has been obtained, that light is deflected in accordance with Einstein's law of gravitation." Even at this dramatic moment, however, one of the distinguished scientists participating in the conference pointed to a portrait of Newton that hung in the meeting hall and

ECLIPSE SHOWED GRAVITY VARIATION

Diversion of Light Rays Accepted as Affecting Newton's Principles.

HAILED AS EPOCHMAKING

British Scientist Calls the Discovery One of the Greatest of Human Achievements.

Copyright, 1919, by The New York Times Company.
Special Cable to THE NEW YORK TIMES.

LONDON, Nov. 8.—What Sir Joseph Thomson, President of the Royal Society, declared was "one of the greatest—perhaps the greatest—of achievements in the history of human thought", was discussed at a joint meeting of the Royal Society and the Royal Astronomical Society in London yesterday, when the results of the British observations of the total solar eclipse of May 29 were made known.

There was a large attendance of astronomers and physicists, and it was generally accepted that the observations were decisive in verifying the prediction of Dr. Einstein, Professor of Physics in the University of Prague, that rays of light from stars, passing close to the sun on their way to the earth, would suffer twice the deflection for which the principles enunciated by Sir Isaac Newton accounted. But there was a difference of opinion as to whether science had to face merely a new and unexplained fact or to reckon with a theory that would completely revolutionize the accepted fundamentals of physics.

The discussion was opened by the Astronomer Royal, Sir Frank Dyson, who described the work of the expeditions sent respectively to Sobral, in Northern Brazil, and the Island of Principe, off the west coast of Africa. At each of these places, if the weather were propitious on the day of the eclipse, it would be possible to take during totality a set of photographs of the obscured sun and a number of bright stars which happened to be in its immediate vicinity.

The desired object was to ascertain whether the light from these stars as it passed by the sun came as directly toward the earth as if the sun were not there, or if there was a deflection due to its presence. And if the deflection did occur the stars would appear on the photographic plates at measurable distances from their theoretical positions. Sir Frank explained in detail the apparatus that had been employed, the corrections that had to be made for various disturbing factors, and the methods by which comparison between the theoretical and observed positions had been made. He convinced the meeting that the results were definite and conclusive, that deflection did take place, and that the measurements showed that the extent of deflection was in close accord with the theoretical degree predicted by Dr. Einstein, as opposed to half of that degree, the amount that would follow if the principles of Newton were correct.

Dr. Crommelin, one of the observers at Sobral, who spoke next, said that eight exposures of twenty-eight seconds each were made during the totality of the eclipse. Seven of these plates showed seven stars in each. One showed no stars, owing to the presence of a thin cloud, but gave well-defined images of the inner corona of the sun and of great prominence. Seven exposures of the same star field were made for comparison between July 14 and July 18 in the morning sky, the sun being then 45 degrees or more away from it. The results reduced to the sun's limb were 2.08 seconds and 1.94 seconds respectively. The combined result was 1.98 seconds, with a probable error of about 6 per cent. This was a strong confirmation of Einstein's theory, which gave a shift at the limb of 1.7 seconds. The evidence in favor of the gravitational bending of light was overwhelming, and there was a decidedly stronger case for the Einstein shift than for the Newtonian one.

Though the results were fairly conclusive, Dr. Crommelin said the question of the revision of Newton's law of gravitation was one of such fundamental importance that consideration was already being given to the next total eclipse in September, 1922, visible in the Maldive Islands and Australia.

Two of the consequences of Einstein's theory, he continued, namely, the motion of Mercury's perihelion and the bending of light by gravitation, might now be looked on as established, "at least with great probability." There was, however, a third predicted consequence, which was a shift of the lines in the spectrum toward the red in a strong gravitational field. The effect in the solar spectrum would amount to one-twentieth of the Angstrum unit, the same as that due to a motion of one-half kilometer per second away from the sun. Dr. St. John had looked for this effect without success. If this failure were taken as final it would mean that parts of Einstein's theory would need revision, but the parts already verified would remain.

The effects on practical astronomy, Dr. Crommelin said, of the verification of Einstein's theory were not very great. It was chiefly in the field of philosophic thought that the change would be felt. Space would no longer be looked on as extending indefinitely in all directions. Euclidian straight lines could not exist in Einstein's space. They would all be curved, and if they traveled far enough they would regain their starting point.

Sir Joseph Thomson, summing up the discussion, said:

"These are not isolated results that have been obtained. It is not the discovery of an outlying island, but of a whole continent of new scientific ideas of the greatest importance to some of the most fundamental questions connected with physics. It is the greatest discovery in connection with gravitation since Newton enunciated that principle."

On November 9, 1919, the New York Times *reported on the proceedings of the Royal Society's meeting in London, in which Einstein's theory regarding the bending of light was confirmed by observations made during a total solar eclipse earlier in the year.*

cautioned his fellow scientists, "We owe it to that great man to proceed very carefully in modifying or retouching his law of gravitation."

Just as the special theory altered our ideas of time and space, the general theory leads to equally astonishing predictions. One startling prediction is that a clock closer to a heavy mass should run more slowly than one farther away from it. A vibrating atom, for example, can be considered to be a clock, sending out pulses of energy at regular intervals. The frequency of the atom's vibration near the sun will therefore be lower than that of the same atom on earth. This shift toward lower frequency and therefore longer wavelength means that light reaching us from the sun will be slightly shifted toward the longer wavelength or red light part of the optical spectrum. This so-called *gravitational red shift* has been experimentally observed and is in satisfactory agreement with the relativity theory.

Another famous prediction from Einstein's theory is the excess precession of the *perihelion* (the distance closest to the sun) of the orbit of Mercury. According to Newton, the orbit of the planet Mercury as it travels around the sun is a perfect ellipse. According to relativity theory, however, the orbit is not quite a closed ellipse. The effect of the strong gravitational field near the sun, or of the "curved space" near the sun, as Einstein would put it, is to cause the perihelion to precess at the rate of about one hundredth of a degree per century. This small discrepancy had already been discovered by astronomers during the nineteenth century, and the agreement with Einstein's theory represented an immediate success for relativity.

SPACE CURVATURE

Perhaps the most startling idea put forward by Einstein in his general theory was the association of gravity with the curvature of space in the neighborhood of a given mass. To make matters worse, he spoke of a *four-dimensional space* that he called "spacetime." It is difficult enough to conceive of a curved three-dimensional space, let alone a curved spacetime. We all learned geometry in school and might be aware that it was called Euclidean. It was named after the Greek mathematician Euclid (about 300 B.C.), who first systematically stated such apparently self-evident axioms as that parallel lines will never meet and then derived various theorems about triangles, circles, and other figures. But the Euclidean geometry we learned at school pertains only to figures that can be drawn on a flat surface, like a tabletop. If the figures are drawn on a curved surface, such as a sphere, Euclid's theorems do not hold. If we were to draw a triangle on the surface of the earth, for example, the sum of the angles would be *greater* than 180 degrees. For a triangle drawn on a surface shaped like a saddle, the sum of the angles would be *less* than 180 degrees. Mathematicians call the curvature of the earth's surface positive and the curvature of the saddle negative.

A possible objection might be that the lines forming the triangles are not straight. They are, however, the straightest lines possible on these surfaces. Mathematicians call such lines geodesic lines, or simply *geodesics.*

Einstein's revolutionary idea was that the presence of a large mass, such as the sun, changed the curvature of the "four-dimensional spacetime continuum" around the sun. His theory gives us the method for determining how matter changes the curvature of spacetime. We all know that light travels in a straight line. A ray of light traveling near the sun is deflected not because of a force but because it is traveling along a straight line (geodesic) in curved spacetime. Similarly, the planets orbit around the sun because they are moving in straight lines (geodesics) in curved spacetime.

The evidence makes it clear that Newtonian mechanics must be modified. As Newton himself said in his *Principia,* "In experimental philosophy we are to look upon propositions obtained by general induction from phenomena as accurately or very nearly

Zero Curvature

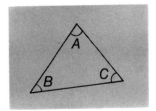

$$A + B + C = 180°$$

Positive Curvature

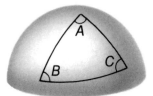

$$A + B + C > 180°$$

Negative Curvature

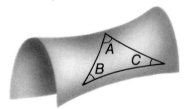

$$A + B + C < 180°$$

true till such times as other phenomena occur, by which they may either be made more accurate, or liable to exceptions.''

GRAVITY WAVES

Einstein's interpretation of gravity involves the concept of a *field*. The gravitational field consists of the deformed spacetime that surrounds an object such as the earth. An apple near the surface of the earth is then not truly in empty space but finds itself immersed in this gravitational field, which acts as an intermediary between the earth and the apple.

This gravitational field has many elements in common with the well-known electromagnetic field surrounding electric charges. The existence of the electric field became apparent in the latter part of the nineteenth century when it was discovered that parts of the field could be transmitted through space in the form of waves. Every time we listen to the radio or turn on our TV, we are receiving electromagnetic waves being transmitted by means of the electromagnetic field. By analogy, then, are there gravity waves?

In a famous paper published in 1918, Einstein did in fact obtain solutions to his relativistic equations that predicted the existence of such waves. These gravitational disturbances were

Facing page: *The sum of the angles A, B, C of a two-dimensional triangle is 180 degrees. If an triangle is drawn on a sphere, the sum would be more than 180 degrees. If a triangle were drawn on a saddle-shaped surface, the sum of the angles would be less than 180 degrees.*

extraordinarily weak and traveled through space with the speed of light.

Detecting such a weak wave presents enormous experimental problems, and no such wave has yet been reliably seen. Serious efforts to observe these waves are being made, however, by such pioneers in gravity-wave research as Joseph Weber and his colleagues at the University of Maryland. He and other scientists have constructed ingenious "antennas" and gravity-wave "telescopes," such as large masses connected by a spring that would oscillate when a ripple in the gravitational field passed by, or large solid cylinders that would be compressed and stretched by the passage of a gravitational wave. Scientists have estimated that the waves are so weak that it would take the shock waves from a cataclysmic cosmic event, such as an exploding star, to be detected. Indirect evidence for the existence of gravity waves, however, comes from observations of a binary star system discovered in 1975 and known officially as PSR 1913 + 16. The system, which consists of a *pulsar* and another star rotating around each other, generates disturbances in the surrounding spacetime that produce waves. These waves carry away energy and produce changes in the motion of the rotating system of stars that should cause them to come closer together. Although some uncertainty exists, the observed loss of energy has so far proven consistent with what would be expected on the assumption that gravity waves are being radiated away from the system.

BLACK HOLES

A *black hole* is a stellar object from which nothing can escape. Its gravitational field is so strong that it can even prevent light from leaving its surface, and so it appears totally black. It is, in effect, invisible.

Black holes are formed by the gravitational collapse of a massive star. All the atoms that make up a star are attracted to the center of the star, so that the star spends its entire life battling the attempt of its own self-gravity to constantly try to make it smaller. The sun, for example, would not be able to maintain its present size against the contracting tendency of its own gravitational force if it were not for the stabilizing pressures built up in its interior by the heat generating thermonuclear reactions. Our sun, and other stars like it, are slow-burning fusion reactors, generating energy by converting hydrogen fuel into helium. The energy source is crucial, not only for keeping us warm and supplying light but for maintaining the counterpressure against the star's massive weight pressing in on itself. If the supply of fuel begins to decrease, the temperature in the star's interior begins to drop and the star begins to contract. As it shrinks and as its matter becomes more and more compact, the force of gravity increases, further upsetting the balance between the two stabilizing opposing forces. The star now begins to contract even faster than before. Eventually, if the star is massive enough, the self-gravity becomes so strong that the star simply collapses.

Do black holes really exist? A collapsed star can be very small indeed, approximately 12 to 19 miles (20–30 km) across, and therefore obviously difficult to locate in the vastness of space. When matter from a companion star becomes trapped and squeezed by the gravitational field of a black hole, however, the gas becomes hot and dense enough, as it rushes toward the black hole, to radiate X-rays before it reaches the region, known as the "event horizon," from which nothing can escape. It should be possible to detect these X-rays.

Since X-rays cannot penetrate the earth's atmosphere, it is necessary to go above the atmosphere with a rocket or a satellite. The first X-ray satellite, named the Uhuru, was launched in 1969 and was very productive. The behavior of two of the most famous X-ray sources it located, Cygnus X-1 and Circinus X-1, convinced astronomers that they had enough evidence to announce in 1973 that a black hole had been discovered. In other attempts to find black holes, their gravitational effect on other stars has been used to detect them, and many candidates have been identified.

The relation between black holes and the universe is based on calculations involving Einstein's general theory of relativity. It is at the forefront of research in astronomy. Future developments and progress in the quantum theory of gravity should bring some surprising and unexpected developments. The gravitational quantum theory, called *supergravity*, will be discussed in chapter 6.

CHAPTER

THE NATURE
OF LIGHT

One of the great unanswered questions in physics has been on the nature of light. Is it a wave or is it a particle? Discussions, experiments, and theories have involved scientists from Newton to Einstein and Planck. In the beginning of the twentieth century, it served as the stimulus for one of the great revolutions in physics, the birth of quantum mechanics.

PARTICLE OR WAVE

Newton was one of the most influential advocates of the early theories of light that considered it to be a stream of particles or corpuscles. He rejected the wave theory because it was observed that light apparently traveled in a straight line. "To me the fundamental supposition itself seems impossible, namely, that the waves or vibrations of any fluid can, like the rays of light, be propagated in straight lines without a continual and very extravagant spreading and bending every way into the quiescent medium, where they are terminated by it. I mistake if there be not both experiment and demonstration to the contrary."

Using the particle theory, Newton could easily explain the laws governing the reflection of light. A stream of particles bouncing off a hard, flat surface would obviously change its

direction. Obeying the laws of mechanics, it would then bounce in such a way that the angle at which it hit the surface would be the same as the angle at which it was reflected. This phenomenon of equal angles was experimentally observed.

The bending of light when it passes from air into water or glass was a bit more difficult to explain. This bending, which is called *refraction*, was visualized by Newton as being caused by the light particles being strongly attracted by the water or the glass. As they approach the surface of a medium such as glass, said Newton, they receive a momentary impulse toward the surface from this attractive force. This force changes the direction of their motion and bends the beam of particles toward the surface. Implied in this theory, however, was the idea that the light particles would travel faster in the water or glass than in air because the force pulling them into the denser materials would add to their velocity.

The chief proponents of the wave theory were the English physicist Robert Hooke (who also clashed with Newton over who should be given priority for first discovering the law of gravity) and the Dutch physicist Christian Huygens. Huygens believed light to be a wave motion propagating through a medium he called "the world ether." Contrary to Newton, he believed that light travels more slowly when it enters a medium denser than air. To explain refraction using the principles of Huygens, one can visualize a wave of light approaching a surface at an angle, like a row of soldiers marching over a grassy field toward a muddy terrain. If the soldiers who first entered the mud are forced to slow down, while those still on the grass maintain their previous marching speed, the whole row will bend toward the mud.

Newton investigating
the properties of light

Because of Newton's great reputation and authority, his particle theory was accepted for more than a century. When Thomas Young showed in 1802 that light exhibits interference effects similar to those of mechanical waves, some doubt began to creep into the scientific world. Later he also discovered diffraction effects in which light appears to bend as it passes sharp corners. It was not until 1850 that the speed of light in water was accurately measured. It was found to be less than the speed in air. Huygens had been right and Newton had been wrong. The wave theory was triumphant and ruled the world of physics, at least until the beginning of the twentieth century.

ELECTROMAGNETIC WAVES

The culmination of the classical theory of light came in 1860, when the great mathematical physicist James Clerk Maxwell published his theory of electromagnetism. Using only a few unifying principles and equations, he demonstrated that light is only a small part of a whole spectrum of electric and magnetic phenomena. The theory predicted the existence of electromagnetic waves, waves that consist of vibrating electric and magnetic fields and that travel through free space with the speed of light. The evidence seems inescapable that light is an electromagnetic wave. Light, X-rays, and radio waves appear at first glance to be quite different. They are all actually the same thing: electromagnetic waves, differing only in the distance between successive wave crests (the wavelength.) Unlike other waves, however, electromagnetic waves do not need a medium to travel through and can propagate themselves through a vacuum.

The theoretical prediction of electromagnetic waves was confirmed in Germany in 1887, when Heinrich Hertz succeeded in transmitting and receiving electromagnetic waves. All our radio, radar, and TV today are proof of the existence of electromagnetic waves. By the end of the nineteenth century, scientists believed that little, if anything, would be added in the future to our knowledge of the nature of light. They were very wrong.

THE PHOTOELECTRIC EFFECT

Among the first hints that the classical wave theory of light had problems was the *photoelectric effect.* It is well known that when light is made to fall on certain metals, electrons are given off by the metal. The emission of these electrons, called photo emission, is rather like the evaporation of water vapor from the surface of liquid water. In both cases, energy is required to allow the electron or water molecule to escape from forces holding them in the nonvapor phase.

At first glance, it seemed easy to explain the effect using the wave theory. A wave, after all, carries energy as it moves through a medium. The electron simply absorbs the energy of the light wave hitting the metal and escapes. The more energy it absorbs, the more energy it should have outside the metal. What was troublesome, however, was that the energy of the escaping electron did not depend on the intensity (or energy) carried by the light. A stronger light did not produce more energetic electrons.

In 1905, the explanation of the photoelectric effect was proposed by Einstein, who said that light energy does not travel in waves but in little bundles or packages he called photons. The energy of each photon is given by the celebrated equation:

$$\text{Energy of photon} = \text{Planck's constant} \times \text{frequency}$$

Planck's constant is named for Max Planck, who, while investigating the radiation given off when an object is heated, first demonstrated that energy could only take on certain values.

Einstein's ideas won him the Nobel Prize and have since become the foundation for the understanding of the interaction of energy and matter. But what of the wave theory? Was Newton right after all?

There can be little doubt that light behaves like a wave when it travels through a given medium. It would be impossible to explain such effects as interference in any other way. But there is also now no doubt that light behaves like a particle, or photon, when it interacts with matter. Light has a dual nature. In the modern view the best we can say is that light is neither a wave nor a particle, but exhibits either wave or particle properties, depending on the experiment you are doing. Although this may seem like no explanation at all, it leads the way into the world of the atom through the development of quantum mechanics. We shall see in Chapter VI how the discovery of the dual nature of light led to the discovery of the dual nature of matter itself.

COLORS AND THE SPECTRUM

Our lives are filled with color, both transmitted and reflected. If we look through a stained glass window, we see beautiful colors of all shades. The light from the sun shining outside has somehow been transformed into colors. Does the glass "add" color to the light? We know from the work of Newton that this is not so, that on the contrary, the glass subtracts colors from the white light passing through it. The color we see is the one that managed to get through.

The study of color is usually associated with prisms and the beautiful bands of colors they produce. Color received its first serious scientific attention, however, in the middle of the seventeenth century when telescopes of high magnification were coming into use. It soon became apparent that most of the images were blurred or ringed with colored fringes. It was almost impossible to get a clear image. The search to eliminate the color distortion or *chromatic aberration*, as it was called, from optical instruments became a major scientific project of the time.

Newton started experimenting with light very early in his student life at Cambridge. In his usual fashion, he polished and made many of his own lenses. "If I had stayed for other people to make my tools and things for me I had never made anything of it," he said later. His famous work on the analysis of white light was begun in 1666, when he managed to find "a Triangular glass-Prisme, to try therewith the celebrated Phenomena of Colours." His brilliant experiments formed the basis of all explanations of the phenomena of color for two centuries to come.

In one such experiment, he allowed a narrow beam of light to fall on a screen in a darkened room. When a prism was placed in the path of the beam, the round image of the beam was replaced by a band of colors. The band, which Newton called a *spectrum*, was red at one end and violet at the other end, with the well-known ordering of orange, yellow, green, and blue spread continuously between them. Others before him had seen the band of colors produced when a beam of sunlight passed through a prism, but they had thought this to be an effect caused in some way by the prism itself. Newton carried his experiments one step further. By allowing the spread of colors to pass through another reversed prism, he found that he could recombine the colors into white again. In the really decisive experiment, the one he called the *experimentum crucis*, or decisive test, he then used an opaque screen with a slit in it to single out one color from the spectrum. When he then passed this color through another prism, he found that it remained unchanged by its passage through the prism.

The refractive index or *refrangibility*, as Newton called it, of light in glass is a number that tells how much light will bend when it passes through the glass. Newton had discovered that a spectrum is formed because, as he put it, "light consists of rays differently refrangible, which were, according to their degrees of refrangibility, transmitted towards divers parts of the wall."

The rainbow is one of the most beautiful natural illustrations of reflection and refraction (bending of light). In a brilliant analysis, Newton showed how light entered a raindrop and after reflec-

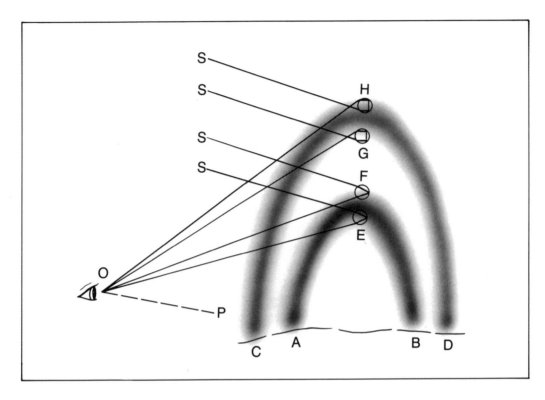

Newton's explanation of a rainbow: "Suppose that O is the spectator's eye, and OP a line drawn parallel to the sun's rays and let POE, POF, POG, and POH be angles of 40 degr. 17 min., 42 degr. 2 min., 50 degr. 57 min., and 54 degr. 7 min., respectively, and these angles turned about their common side OP, shall with their other sides OE, OF, OG, and OH describe the verges of two rainbows AF, BE, and CHDG. For if E, F, G, and H be drops placed anywhere in the conical [surfaces] described by OE, OF, OG, and OH, and be illuminated by the sun's rays SE, SF, SG, and SH; the angle SEO being equal to the angle POE, or 40 degr. 17 min., shall be the greatest angle in which the most refrangible rays can after one reflection be refracted to the eye, and therefore all the drops in the line OE shall send the most refrangible rays most copiously to the eye, and thereby strike the sense with the deepest violet color in that region."

tion was again refracted as it left the drop. The water behaved exactly like the glass prism and separated the sunlight into the spectrum of colors.

If we now ask why grass is green, the answer is that the grass contains a pigment that absorbs most colors, leaving only green to be reflected. The sky is blue because the air molecules permit all other colors to pass through it while preferentially scattering blue light back to earth.

THE REFLECTING TELESCOPE

Was it possible to eliminate the persistent color fringes that distorted images in optical instruments such as telescopes? On the basis of his experiments in optics, Newton concluded that because of refraction, a telescope made with lenses would always show chromatic aberration. He was both right and wrong. If a lens is made of one kind of glass only, Newton was correct. We have learned, however, that it is possible to correct for color distortion by using several different kinds of glass and combining them into one lens.

Newton promptly set to work to make a new kind of telescope, one without a large collecting lens. The light-gathering would be accomplished by means of a reflecting concave mirror instead of a lens. When light is reflected from a mirror, all the colors reflect at the same angle. Newton cast and ground the metal mirror from an alloy that he prepared himself. He built the tube and the mount. The telescope was about 6 inches (15 cm) long, but it magnified nearly forty times in diameter. To view the image, Newton cleverly put a small mirror tilted at 45 degrees to the path of light to direct the focus out of the side of the telescope tube, where an eyepiece was placed.

When the telescope was shown to the Royal Society, it created a sensation. Even Newton's rival, the Dutch physicist Huygens, called it "the marvellous telescope of Mr. Newton."

A reflecting telescope's size is denoted by the size of its light-gathering mirror. Newton's telescope had a mirror whose diameter was about 1 inch (2.54 cm); it is therefore called a 1-inch reflector. All large telescopes built now are reflectors. The largest in the United States today is the 200-inch (5-m) reflector at Mount Palomar in California. The largest telescope in the world is a new 236-inch (6-m) reflector built in the Soviet Union that began operating in 1976. Most of the newer telescopes being built throughout the world are substantially smaller than this. Large telescopes permit astronomers to peer deep into space. Billions of new galaxies have been discovered, as well as unexpected stellar objects such as pulsars and quasars. These powerful telescopes enable us to see beyond the small realm of the solar system into a vast, restless universe.

RADIO ASTRONOMY

Astronomers have long thought that if they could examine space through eyes sensitive to other parts of the electromagnetic spectrum, such as radio waves or X-rays, it would completely alter the appearance of the night sky. Radio astronomy was born in 1930, when Karl Jansky identified the Milky Way as a source of radio noise. During World War II, scientists in England discovered that the sun was occasionally a strong emitter of radio waves. The floodgates were open for a new way of exploring the sky.

A radio telescope functions like a reflecting telescope. A large dish reflects incoming radio signals to a focus, where the concentrated radiation is detected by a radio receiver instead of the eye of an observer. It can be used both day and night and even on cloudy days. Because radio telescopes do not require large mas-

The world's most powerful radio telescope, the Very Large Array, is located west of Socorro, New Mexico.

sive mirrors that often sag under their own weight, they can be made much larger than optical telescopes, with more radiation-catching ability and more sensitivity.

Because it deals with radio waves rather than light waves, a radio telescope does have a drawback. Radio waves are longer than light waves, and therefore a radio telescope cannot distinguish the distance between two closely placed points in space as well as an optical instrument. Its *resolution* is poorer. This is usually overcome by using several telescopes in an array and synchronizing their signals. The largest such system, called the Very Large Array (VLA), is in New Mexico.

The first source of radio waves outside our solar system was discovered in 1946. It appeared to be located in the constellation of Cygnus and was accordingly named Cygnus A. To astronomers, it supplied evidence that cosmic rays, that mysterious form of radiation emanating from space, originate in exploding galaxies. At last count, more than 4,000 radio sources have been mapped. Among the powerful radio sources in the sky are quasars, or quasi-stellar objects. These starlike objects have been shown to be receding from the earth at velocities comparable to the most distant galaxies in the universe. They were small, yet they seemed to radiate enormous amounts of energy, in some cases as much as forty times as much energy as a typical large galaxy containing 100 billion stars. The question of the nature of quasars and the source of this energy is still open; it is one of the outstanding problems of astrophysics.

Another one of the surprises that radio astronomers stumbled onto was the pulsar. A group at the University of Cambridge in England, operating a new radio telescope, noticed a very weak source of radio signals coming from a point among the stars that produced, in the words of one astronomer, "a succession of pulses as regularly spaced as a broadcast time service." These pulses were first thought to be electrical interference or even, in a more imaginative moment, some message from outer space. "Little green men" were jokingly invented as the originators of these pulses. More than several hundred pulsars have now been studied in detail. Since the discovery of the famous pulsar in the Crab Nebula in 1968, pulsars have been identified as rotating neutron stars that are remnants of gigantic stellar explosions called *supernovas.*

Radio astronomy's most astonishing discovery, however, was the detection of the background radiation that fills the entire universe. This discovery was accidentally made in 1965 by Arno A. Penzias and Robert W. Wilson of the Bell Telephone Laboratories in New Jersey, while they were attempting to calibrate one of the first satellite communications telescopes. They were later awarded the Nobel Prize for their achievement. This primordial background radiation was later identified as a remnant of the *big bang,* the explosive moment of the creation of the universe. It represents almost conclusive evidence for the validity of the "big bang" theory, as we shall see in the next chapter.

SATELLITE ASTRONOMY

The atmosphere of the earth blocks out most of the radiation reaching the earth. Only visible light and radio waves manage to enter through the two rather small "windows" of the electromagnetic spectrum that the surrounding air does not absorb. The ability to put telescopes in orbit above the atmosphere of the earth made it possible to observe the sky in radically new ways. Stars, galaxies, pulsars, and quasars could now be examined by observing their ultraviolet and X-ray emission, regions of the spectrum never before seen by astronomers. The Orbiting Astronomical Observatory (OAO–II), placed in orbit in December 1968, provided information about the ultraviolet output of more than 50,000 stars.

The most widely used telescope now available to astronomers is known as IUE, the International Ultraviolet Explorer, launched in 1978. It uses a television-type device called a *vidicon* as a detector, and it supplies data to hundreds of astronomers in

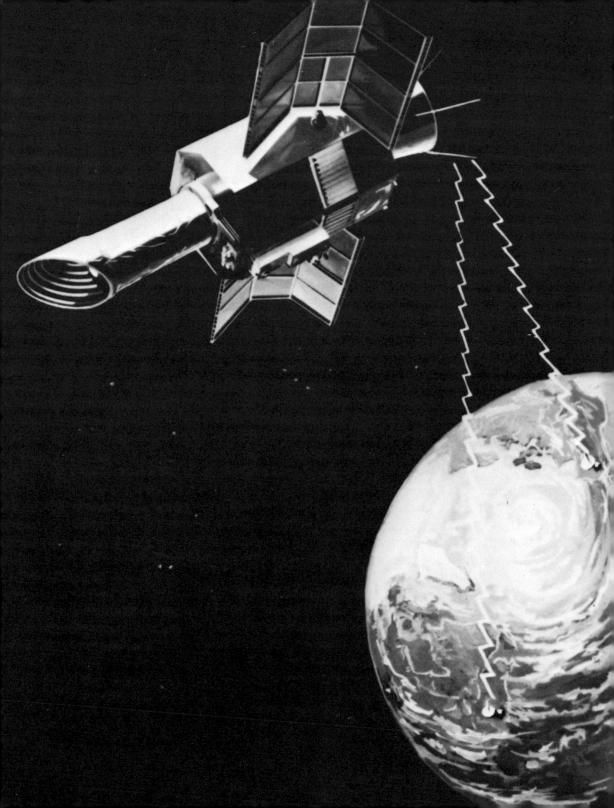

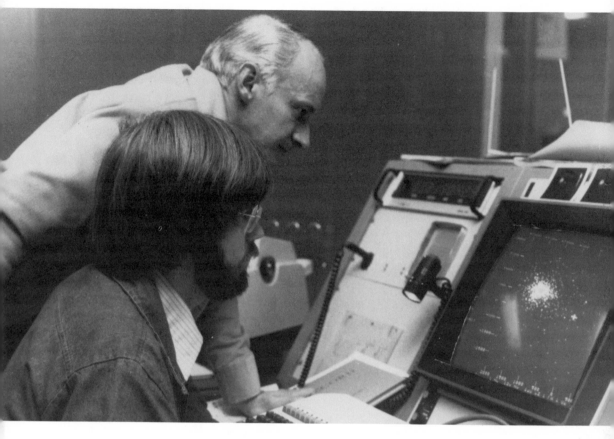

Facing Page: *the IUE (International Ultraviolet Explorer) was launched in 1978. It is in synchronous orbit with the earth, transmitting and receiving information from the Goddard Space Flight Center in Greenbelt, Maryland, and the European Space Agency's station near Madrid, Spain. Above: scientists watch a viewing screen at the Goddard Space Flight Center as an image of the first star observed by the IUE appears. The IUE is designed to study a wide range of celestial objects in the ultraviolet region of the spectrum, largely inaccessible to ground-based telescopes.*

the United States. The telescope was built by NASA and is controlled from the Goddard Space Flight Center in Maryland.

An astronomer can ask NASA to look at a certain star and can then observe the image on a television screen in the Goddard control room. A choice is usually first made as to what region in the ultraviolet is to be investigated. The telescope operator then takes an exposure whose results are again displayed on a TV screen. Within seconds, computers can plot graphs and display any part of the spectrum that the astronomer desires.

The IUE has been a tremendous success. Newton, with his love for well-made equipment, would have relished the transition from the laborious tracing of emulsions on photographic plates used in conventional telescopes to computerized telescopes on spacecraft.

Planned for the future is a new Space Telescope, to be launched from the Space Shuttle. It will concentrate on studies in the visible and ultraviolet regions of the spectrum. It is expected that every few years astronauts can visit the Space Telescope with the Space Shuttle to make repairs and change scientific instruments. It will allow us to see objects seven times farther away than we can now. Our understanding of many astronomical phenomena will be vastly improved.

CHAPTER

NEWTON AND COSMOLOGY

One of Newton's most ambitious applications of his theory of universal gravitation was trying to understand how the universe was formed. In a letter written to Richard Bentley on December 10, 1692, Newton posed one of the important questions of cosmology: Why don't all the stars draw themselves together into one huge ball? "It seems to me," he said, "that if the matter of our Sun and Planets and all the matter in the Universe was evenly scattered throughout all the heavens, and every particle had an innate gravity towards all the rest . . . and if the whole space throughout which this matter was scattered was but finite, the matter on the outside of the space would by its gravity tend towards all the matter on the inside and by its consequence . . . compose one great spherical mass."

We have already seen that gravitational collapse plays a key role in black hole and star formation. In the case of stars, nuclear reactions produce high internal pressures that oppose the tendency of self-gravity to compress the stellar mass. In the phenomenon of black holes, a gravitational collapse does indeed occur, producing a ball of matter so dense that not even light can escape from it. The galaxies themselves show signs of gravitational collapse, with much of the original gas and dust collected into globular clusters of stars.

But what about the universe? Is it static and unchanging or will it also collapse? Is it finite or infinite? Newton's questions have been revived and have become some of the leading problems of modern cosmology.

HUBBLE'S LAW

In 1929, Edwin Hubble, an astronomer at the Mount Wilson Observatory in California, made one of the most astonishing discoveries of our century. He found that galaxies in every direction were moving away from us. It appeared that the entire universe was expanding.

Hubble observed that light coming from galaxies exhibits a *red shift*. That is, all the colors are shifted toward the red end, the longer-wavelength part, of the spectrum. This shift in light from a receding galaxy resembles the Doppler shift that is heard in the sound of a horn being blown by a car moving away from us. In both cases, the wavelength will appear to increase, resulting in a drop in pitch in the case of the car and a color shift toward red in the case of the galaxy. The expansion of the universe in every direction around us does not imply that we are at the center of the universe. Imagine a balloon with spots painted over its entire surface being blown up. As the balloon gets larger, the distance between any two adjacent spots increases, yet there is no spot that is in the "center" of the expansion.

Hubble also found another remarkable property of these galaxies. The farther they are away from us, the greater the red shift is, and therefore the faster they are receding. The velocity increases in strict proportion to the distance. Because of this, a

Edwin Hubble was the first astronomer to discover that the entire universe is expanding.

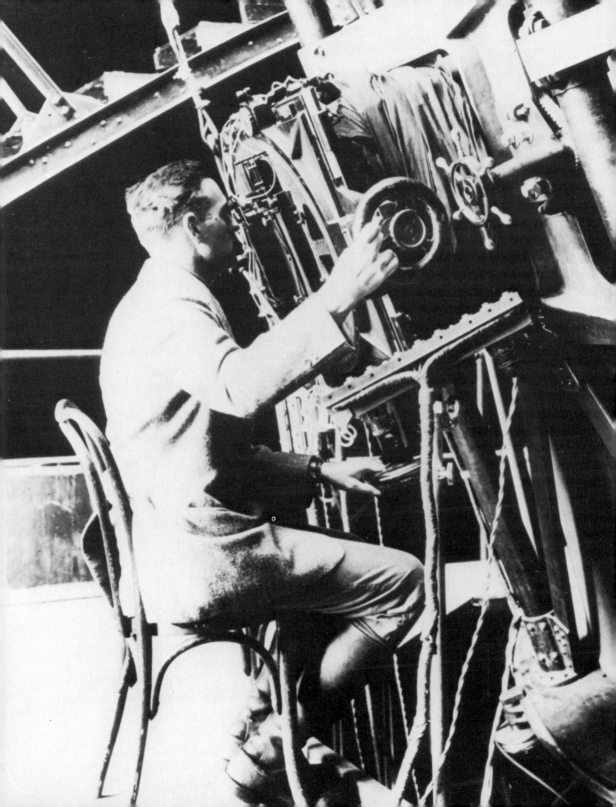

constant ratio of distance to velocity can be calculated. The ratio is such that a galaxy that is 1 million light-years (one light-year is the distance light travels in one year) from us recedes with a velocity of 11 miles (17 km) per second; another galaxy twice as far away recedes twice as fast, or 22 miles (34 km) per second, and so on. This is known as *Hubble's law.*

THE BIG BANG

The universe is expanding. It is apparent, then, that all the galaxies that are now flying apart must have at one time been closer together. There must have been some unique moment in the past when all the matter in the universe was squeezed into a small region of almost infinite density. This state represents the big bang, and it marks the origin of the universe. Space and time were created in that event, and so was all the matter in the universe. We can trace the expansion backward in time and calculate how long ago it all began. This time, called *Hubble time*, is now thought to be approximately 19 or 20 billion years.

Just as a ball falls back to earth unless it is thrown with sufficient speed, the galaxies we see receding from each other in spite of attractive gravitational forces must have been hurled apart in a gigantic cosmic explosion. The debris we see all around us in the form of background radiation is compelling evidence for the big bang. As previously mentioned in our discussion of radio astronomy, two Bell Telephone scientists, Penzias and Wilson, discovered cosmic radiation in the radio region, a remnant of the primordial fireball, that fits perfectly into the framework of the big bang theory.

THE CREATION OF MATTER

In the beginning there was an explosion. How did this fantastic event create the universe we know? Astronomers have been able to develop step-by-step details of the evolution of the universe and to speak meaningfully about the first few seconds of an event that occurred billions of years ago. At first the universe had a fantastically high temperature, about 100 billion degrees Centigrade. Only photons of light and matter in the form of a few so-called elementary particles could have existed in this environment. These particles, with exotic names such as pions, hyperons, protons, neutrons, electrons, neutrinos, and positrons were created out of energy. The concept of particle creation from energy comes directly from Einstein's $E = mc^2$.

After about a hundred seconds, the universe had cooled to a few billion degrees, and the temperature was now low enough for the nuclei of the simplest atoms to form. In addition to hydrogen, heavy hydrogen (deuterium) and helium nuclei were now being created by reactions that can now be duplicated in modern laboratories. At the end of the first few minutes, the temperatures dropped to about 100 million degrees, and there was no longer enough energy available to continue the process of nuclei creation or *nucleosynthesis*, as it is called. About 25 to 30 percent of the matter in the universe had been converted into helium. Nearly all the rest was, and still is, hydrogen. Almost all the helium in the universe, then, was formed within the first five minutes after the big bang. Much later, after many thousands of years, the universe had cooled sufficiently for electrons to combine with the nuclei and form atoms of hydrogen and helium gas. Under the influence of gravity, these gases eventually condensed to form galaxies and stars. The heavier elements, formed at a much later time, are thought to have been synthesized in the interiors of stars.

A SEA OF BUBBLES

The influence of gravity as the primary force in forming galaxies has recently been questioned. A group of scientists from Princeton and Johns Hopkins Universities have suggested that the organization of stars into galaxies may have been set off by shock waves resulting from huge explosions, and not solely by the force of gravity. This idea is supported by the discovery that large regions of the universe are empty of galaxies. The voids appear similar to huge bubbles with galaxies distributed on their surfaces. To quote a member of the research team, "if we are right, these bubbles fill the universe just like suds filling the kitchen sink."

UNIFIED FIELD THEORY

The conception of the early universe that astronomers have developed has shed light on other problems in physics. We know that there exist four fundamental forces in nature: the force of gravity, the electromagnetic force between electrically charged particles, the "strong" force that is responsible for binding together the particles that make up the nuclei of atoms, and the "weak" force that is responsible for certain types of radioactivity. Until quite recently, these forces appeared to be different in almost every respect. Many scientists, the most famous among them being Einstein, felt that nature had in some way disguised these forces and that in reality they were all manifestations of a single, basic interaction. Einstein hoped to bridge the gap between these forces and construct a *unified field theory* of all the physical interactions. The unsuccessful search for the unifying principle occupied him until the end of his life.

In the 1960s, Steven Weinberg and Abdus Salam succeeded in unifying the electromagnetic and "weak" forces. They discovered that these two seemingly different forces derived from a single force when observed at high energies. These energies correspond to the temperature of the universe during the first fraction of a second after the big bang. Other theories have been developed (gauge theories) that unite the "strong" force with the "weak" and electromagnetic forces at still higher energies. It is hoped that if the energy is high enough, it will be possible to extend the theory to include gravity. There would then finally be one grand unification theory for all the forces of nature. The success of the Weinberg-Salam theory has led scientists to believe that at the moment of creation, there was only one universal force. As the universe aged and cooled, a process called *symmetry breaking* occurred that separated this one force into the four we know today.

A new theory called *supergravity* has been developed recently that is even more ambitious. It attempts, by setting up certain symmetry classes of elementary particles, not only to apply quantum theory to gravity but also to unify all the particles of nature as well as the forces. While still in its infancy, it may be a theory that has the power to describe the past, present, and future of the entire physical world.

THE FUTURE OF THE UNIVERSE

Is it possible to predict the eventual fate of the universe? Will the universe expand forever and be what astronomers call an *open universe*, or will it be a *closed universe* and eventually collapse into "a big crunch"? We know that it is expanding now, but will it do so forever? One thing we can be certain of is that because of the gravitational attraction among all galaxies and matter in the universe, the rate of expansion must be slowing down. Is the gravity strong enough to completely overcome the expansion so that the receding galaxies will stop, reverse their motion, and eventually collapse?

The answer is straightforward. If the density of matter in the universe is great enough, the gravitational attraction will be strong enough to stop the expansion. A search for the necessary mass has given inconclusive results. Calculations and observations seem to indicate that the quantity of matter in the universe is too small by a factor of one hundred to halt the expansion. There are many places, however, where undetected mass could be hiding. There could be black holes that are invisible to us, or neutrinos, or molecular hydrogen in space that is difficult to detect. Some astronomers think that as much as 90 percent of the matter in the universe is "dark matter," matter that has eluded detection.

The major method now in use to measure the density of matter in the universe involves an assessment of the abundance of light elements. We have seen that almost all the deuterium and helium were formed during the early moments following the big bang. If we can find out what the density was then, by knowing the age of the universe and its rate of expansion, we can determine what the density is now. Studies using the Copernicus satellite to detect some of these light elements in interstellar space all agree that there is still not enough matter in the universe to stop the expansion. The universe apparently is eternal and not destined to collapse into itself in "a big crunch."

GLOSSARY

Big bang—a model of the universe in which all matter, space, and time, began with a gigantic cosmic explosion of enormous density and pressure, and resulted in the observed expansion of the universe.

Black hole—a gravitationally collapsed mass whose gravitational attraction is so great that nothing, not even light, can escape from its surface.

Chromatic aberration—The distortion of the image formed by a lens, caused by each color of the spectrum coming to a different focus.

Dynamics—the study of the motion of bodies when they are acted upon by various forces.

Electromagnetic force—the force exerted by one particle on another due solely to the electric charges carried by the particles.

Four-dimensional space—a convenient abstraction used to express the results of Einstein's relativity theory. Events are regarded as occurring in a four-dimensional space consisting of the usual three dimensional space coordinates and a fourth coordinate that refers to time.

General theory of relativity—an attempt made by Albert Einstein to express the laws of physics in such a way that they are valid in all frames of reference, regardless of their states of motion. An important postulate of the theory is that in a closed laboratory it is impossible for an observer to distinguish between the effects produced by gravity and those produced by an acceleration of the laboratory.

Geodesic—the shortest line that can be drawn between two points on any surface.

Gravitation—the name given to the force of attraction between any two masses in the universe. It was first described by Sir Isaac Newton in 1687.

Half-life—the amount of time required for any given amount of radioactive material to decrease to half its original activity.

Hubble's law—as the universe expands, it is found that there is a direct correlation between the distance of a galaxy from the earth and its speed of recession: the more distant a galaxy, the faster it is moving.

Inverse-square law—the behavior of certain forces, such as the gravitational or electromagnetic force of attraction between two objects, that decreases as the square of the distance between them.

Length contraction—a phenomenon associated with the special theory of relativity. The length of an object that is measured when moving with respect to a stationary observer appears to be smaller, or to contract in the direction of its motion, when measured by the stationary observer.

Nucleosynthesis—the creation of the atomic nuclei of the heavy elements by nuclear reactions taking place in the interior of stars.

Perihelion—the distance of closest approach to the sun of a planet moving about the sun in an elliptical orbit.

Photoelectric effect—the emission of electrons from a metal surface when light of sufficiently high frequency falls upon it.

Pulsar—a rotating, magnetized, neutron star that emits pulses of radio waves with a very high degree of regularity.

Red shift—the shift toward the longer wavelength, or red, part of the spectrum, of light emitted from a receding source. The light from distant galaxies is red shifted, implying that they are moving away from the earth.

Refraction—the bending of light as it passes from one medium to another.

Special theory of relativity—the theory developed in 1905 by Albert Einstein that analyzes the physical consequences implied by the absence of a universal frame of reference. The theory is based on two postulates. The first states that the laws of physics are the same for all observers in all frames of reference moving at constant velocity with respect to one another. The second states that the speed of light has the same value for all observers, regardless of their state of motion.

Supergravity—a theory that attempts to unify all the forces of nature, including gravity.

Supernova—an enormous stellar explosion in which all but the inner core of a star is blown off into interstellar space. An enormous amount of energy is produced, more in a few days than our sun has radiated in a billion years.

Time dilation—a phenomenon associated with the special theory of relativity. The time interval between two events measured in any system moving with respect to a stationary observer appears to be smaller than when the time interval is measured with the system at rest. Often stated as "a moving clock runs slow."

Trajectory—the path of a moving object.

Unified field theory—the name given to the early attempt by Albert Einstein to unify the forces of nature. Physicists now believe that such a union of all four forces is near, and that supergravity will provide the answer.

Universal gravitation—the name given to the force of gravity to emphasize its universality. It is gravity that binds us to the earth and that binds the planets to the solar system. Gravity plays an important role in the evolution of stars and in the behavior of galaxies.

Velocity—An important concept in the study of motion. The important distinction between velocity and speed is that velocity describes not only how fast an object is moving, but also its direction of motion.

INDEX

ABOUT THE AUTHORS

Eve Stwertka teaches writing and literature at the State University of New York at Farmingdale. A Fulbright Fellow, she holds a doctorate from St. John's University.

Albert Stwertka, her husband, is a physicist. In addition to heading the mathematics and science department at Kings Point, the federal maritime academy on Long Island, New York, he is an accomplished violinist who plays in many chamber music groups.

Together the Stwertkas have written a number of books for Franklin Watts, including *Marijuana*; *Industrial Pollution: Poisoning Our World*; and *Population: Growth, Change, and Impact*.